TABLETOP WARS
BREAK THE SIEGE
Make Your Own Catapults

Thanks to the creative team:
Senior Editor: Alice Peebles
Fact checking: Kate Mitchell
Design: www.collaborate.agency

Hungry Tomato™
A division of Lerner Publishing Group, Inc.
241 First Avenue North
Minneapolis, MN 55401 USA

For reading levels and more information,
look up this title at www.lernerbooks.com.

Main body text set in Bodoni 72.
Typeface provided by International Typeface Corp.

Library of Congress Cataloging-in-Publication Data

Names: Ives, Rob, author. | De Quay, John Paul, illustrator.
Title: Break the Siege : Make Your Own Catapults / Rob Ives ;
John Paul de Quay (illustrator).
Description: Minneapolis : Hungry Tomato, [2016] | Series:
Tabletop wars | Audience: Ages 8–12. | Audience: Grades 4
to 6. | Includes index.
Identifiers: LCCN 2016008882 (print) | LCCN
2016012727 (ebook) | ISBN 9781512406382 (lb : alk.
paper) | ISBN 9781512411720 (pb : alk. paper) | ISBN
9781512409253 (eb pdf)
Subjects: LCSH: Catapult—Juvenile literature. | Weapons—
Juvenile literature. | Sieges—Juvenile literature.
Classification: LCC U875 .I94 2016 (print) | LCC U875
(ebook) | DDC 623.4/41—dc23

0760

LC record available at http://lccn.loc.gov/2016008882

Manufactured in the United States of America
1-39311-21148-5/13/2016

TABLETOP WARS
BREAK THE SIEGE
Make Your Own Catapults

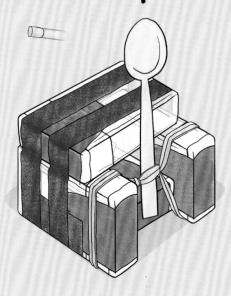

by Rob Ives

Illustrated by John Paul de Quay

HUNGRY
TOMATO™
Minneapolis

Safety First!

Take care and use good sense when making your own siege engines. Even though the models are small, and you may use soft missiles with the siege engines, the unexpected can happen. Be responsible and always be safe.

Bolts, darts, and other missiles can cause damage when fired with force. Never point the siege engines or aim anything at people, animals, or anything of value.

Look for the safety warning sign in the activities and ask an adult for assistance when you are cutting materials.

Watch for this sign throughout the book. You may need help from an adult to complete these tasks.

CONTENTS

SIEGE ENGINES

This book shows you how to make small, fun working models of six mighty siege engines from the ancient days of warfare and beyond. Put them together and launch marshmallows or grapes!

Supply List:

To make the amazing siege engines in this book, you will need these supplies. Most items can be found at home, school, or a craft store:

Cardboard Tube

Large Wooden Skewers

Mesh Bath Sponge

Netting from a Fruit Bag

Plastic Bag

Washcloth

Wooden Spoon

Mini Marshmallows

Wooden Craft Sticks

Pencils

Ballpoint Pen

Rubber Bands

Long Paper Clips, 2 inches (5 cm)

Plastic Cable Ties

Plastic Spoons or Sporks

Plastic Mint Boxes

D-size Battery

Pencil with Eraser

Siege Engines

This is a fun guide to making miniature siege engines from everyday items. The devices that inspired these models come from different historic times, but are mainly early or medieval inventions. All used different methods of shooting a projectile at an enemy or their defenses. These mini-versions deliver grapes. marshmallows, or candy across the room!

So, dig into your drawers and cabinets for the few items you will need, and exercise your fingers and brain. And remember, before you start, to read the safety information on page 4. And look out for the safety warning signs in the activities for steps where you'll need a little adult help. So get ready, get set, and launch!

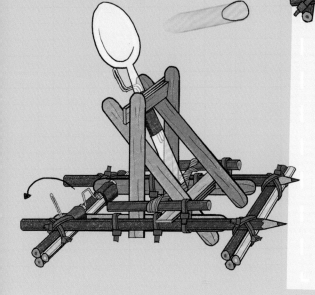

TIPS

Some projects need pencils to be cut into sections. Ask for help with this and use a cutting mat to cut on. An efficient way to do it is to cut each face of the pencil in turn, and then snap it apart. Tidy up any unevenness with a knife.

Also ask for help with cutting the barrel of a pen—this can be quite tricky! One way of doing it neatly is to use a file to make a notch all the way around the barrel and then snap off the piece.

Use pliers to straighten out and shape paper clips.

Tools Needed:

 Craft Knife

 Scissors

 Nail File

 Ruler

 Small Clamp

 Duct Tape

Small Craft Drill   Rubber Bands   Wood Glue   Epoxy Glue   Pliers   String

TREBUCHET

This model is a replica of one of the mightiest medieval weapons, capable of destroying besieged castles. Build this and use it to shoot grapes or similar missiles across your table to destroy your enemy.

Supplies:

Pencils x 5

Plastic Cable Ties x 9

Long Paper Clips x 4

D-size Battery

Wooden Craft Sticks x 13

Large Wooden Skewer

2.8 inches (7 cm)
1.4 inches (3.5 cm)
Mark these measurements on three more craft sticks.

3 inches (8 cm)
2 inches (5 cm)
Netting from a Fruit Bag, cut to 3 x 2 inches (8 x 5 cm)

Tools:

Ruler

Pliers

Craft Knife

Wood Glue

Epoxy Glue

Small Craft Drill

Small Clamp or Rubber Bands

String

Instructions
STAGE 1

1 Scrape the paint from the ends of four pencils, so that glue will stick to them. Place them on a flat surface and glue on two craft sticks with wood glue (as shown).

Tie the pencil tops together tightly with cable ties. Trim the tie ends.

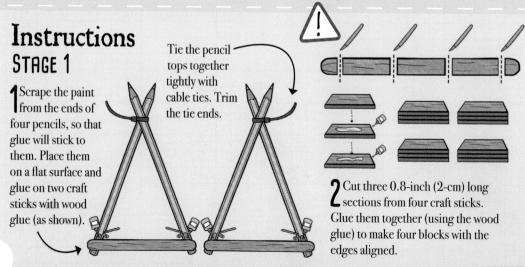

2 Cut three 0.8-inch (2-cm) long sections from four craft sticks. Glue them together (using the wood glue) to make four blocks with the edges aligned.

3 Glue the blocks to the inside of the stretchers, as shown on both ends.

4 Shave off two flat areas below the ties (as shown). Apply glue to these areas. Take the three marked craft sticks shown on page 8.

5 Glue two of the marked craft sticks across the base using the pencil marks for alignment. Glue the third stick across the top. Clamp or hold in place with rubber bands until the glue is completely dry.

6 Place another craft stick at the center lines of the crosspieces. Glue in place. Glue two craft sticks on either side. Glue two craft sticks along their edges to make a trough. This completes the stand.

STAGE 2

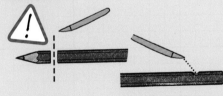

7 Carefully cut the sharp end off the pencil. Cut a notch 0.8 inch (2 cm) from the end of the pencil.

8 Cut the skewer to 5 inches (12.5 cm) long. Apply wood glue to the notch, fit the skewer in place, and secure tightly with two cable ties.

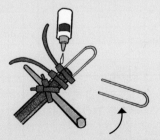

9 Fold 3 inches (8 cm) of paper clip wire into a loop that fits snugly over the pencil end, extending by 0.6 inch (1.5 cm). Fix on the loop with epoxy glue and secure with two cable ties. Trim the ties.

10 Straighten out a paper clip and fold it to make a prong. Place the prong on one side of the pencil at the other end from the skewer, so it extends by 0.5 inch (1 cm).

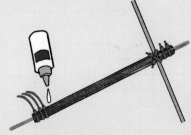

11 Glue the prong in place with epoxy glue. Secure it in place with three cable ties. This is the swinging arm of the trebuchet.

STAGE 3

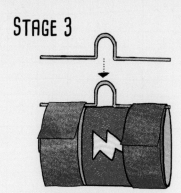

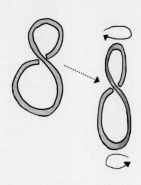

12 Make the top shape from another paper clip. Tape the wire to the middle of the battery to make a hanging loop.

13 Make a flat figure-eight shape from another paper clip. Twist it in the middle and fit it to the hanging loop.

14 Fit the other end to the loop on the swinging arm.

STAGE 4

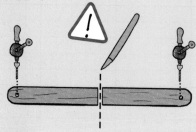

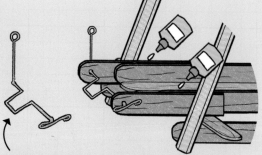

15 Cut a craft stick in half and drill a small hole using the craft drill in the end of each piece. Straighten out a paper clip.

16 Make up the complicated wire shape shown from the paper clip, while threading it through the holes in the craft sticks. This forms the trigger. Glue the craft sticks to the sides of the trough.

STAGE 5

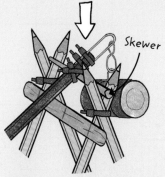

Skewer

17 Thread a short length of string through each end of the netting and tie with a knot as shown. Pull tight and trim off any excess netting to neaten.

18 Drop the skewer crosspiece into the V-shapes made by the pencils in the stand. The battery weight should face the back, on the same side as the trigger.

19 Tie one of the strings to the top of the swing arm. Make an open-ended loop on the other string, so that the two strings are the same length. This is the sling.

20 Hook the string loop over the wire prong on the end of the swing arm. Pull the arm down and engage the trigger. Place a grape missile in the sling at the far end of the trough.

Ready! Aim! Launch!

Pull the trigger back to release the arm of the trebuchet.

MEDIEVAL TREBUCHET

The trebuchet was a powerful siege attack weapon, similar to a catapult, used for hurling heavy stones to smash castle or city walls. It fired its ammunition from great distances. Enemies were often bombarded with other nasty items such as diseased cattle and the severed heads of captives.

11

Onager

Invented by the Romans in roughly 400 BCE, the onager was sometimes so large it had to be assembled on the field of battle. This onager is the perfect size for flinging grapes at your enemy!

Supplies:

Rubber Bands x 2

Netting from a Fruit Bag, cut to 3 x 2 inches (8 x 5 cm)

Wooden Craft Sticks x 7

Long Paper Clips x 4

Plastic Cable Ties x 4

The frame for this model is made from craft sticks and pencils. Cut seven craft stick lengths of 2 inches (5 cm) with heavy scissors.

2 inches (5 cm)

Tools:

Nail File

Duct Tape

String

Scissors

Craft Knife

Epoxy Glue

Pliers

4 inches (10 cm)

3 inches (7.5 cm)

You will need five pencils. Use two at full-length, cut one to 4 inches (10 cm) long, and cut two to 3 inches (7.5 cm).

Instructions
STAGE 1

2 Straighten out a paper clip, fold it around, and make a prong.

1 Glue the craft stick lengths back-to-back to make two pieces of double-thickness. Shape grooves in the ends of the double craft sticks using a nail file.

3 To make the swing arm, take one of the 4-inch (10-cm) pencils and tape the prong to it with duct tape.

STAGE 2

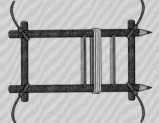

4 Double-up two rubber bands and loop them around the two full-length pencils, one-third of the way along. Fit the two craft stick parts 0.6 inch (1.5 cm) on either side. Glue in place with epoxy glue.

5 Fasten the two 3-inch (7.5-cm) cross pencils to the ends of the long ones using cable ties. Pull tight. Trim the tie ends.

6 Fit the swing arm into the rubber bands and make a couple of turns with it to tighten the bands.

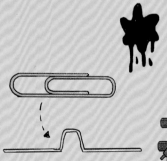

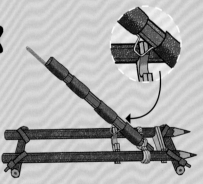

7 Cut a notch in the inner crosspiece so that the swing arm can fit into it.

8 Make a trigger loop from a piece of paper clip wire.

9 Tape the trigger loop to the swing arm so that the loop lines up with the back of the crosspiece.

STAGE 3

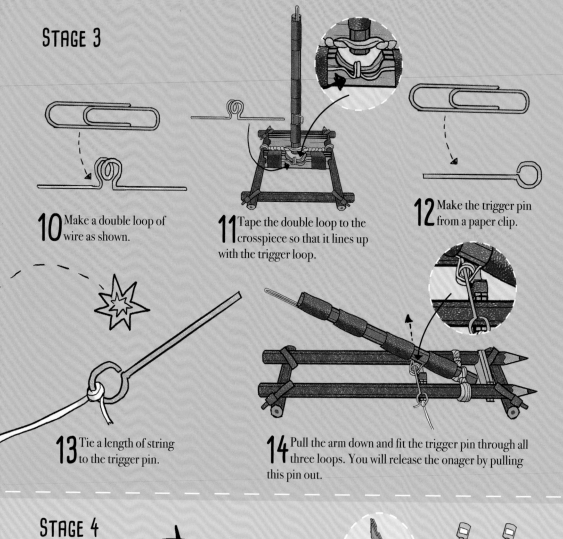

10 Make a double loop of wire as shown.

11 Tape the double loop to the crosspiece so that it lines up with the trigger loop.

12 Make the trigger pin from a paper clip.

13 Tie a length of string to the trigger pin.

14 Pull the arm down and fit the trigger pin through all three loops. You will release the onager by pulling this pin out.

STAGE 4

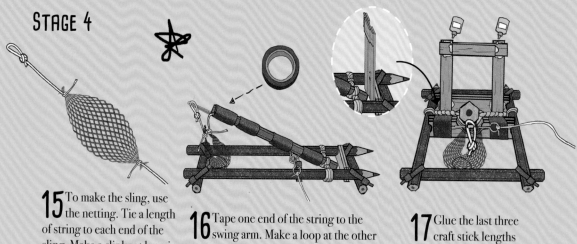

15 To make the sling, use the netting. Tie a length of string to each end of the sling. Make a slipknot loop in one end.

16 Tape one end of the string to the swing arm. Make a loop at the other end to hook over the prong, so that the grape hangs just above the tabletop.

17 Glue the last three craft stick lengths with wood glue as shown, to make two uprights and a crosspiece.

STAGE 5

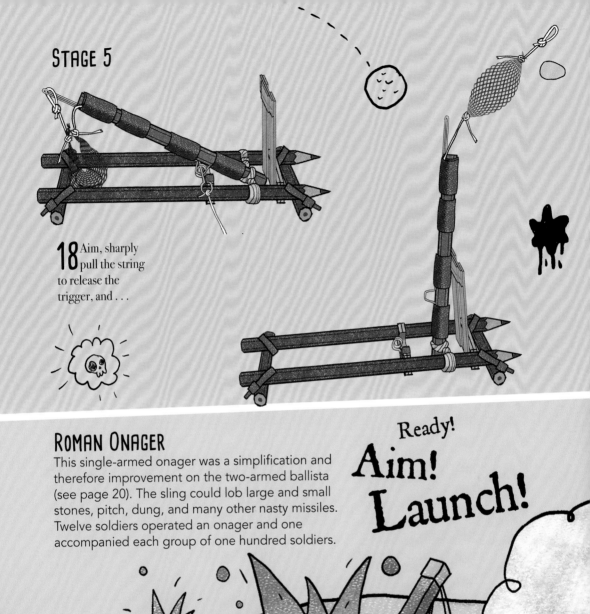

18 Aim, sharply pull the string to release the trigger, and . . .

ROMAN ONAGER

This single-armed onager was a simplification and therefore improvement on the two-armed ballista (see page 20). The sling could lob large and small stones, pitch, dung, and many other nasty missiles. Twelve soldiers operated an onager and one accompanied each group of one hundred soldiers.

Ready!
Aim!
Launch!

CATAPULT

It's amazing what you can do with a spring-mounted spoon, modeled after the medieval catapult. Overpower your enemy with a bombardment of grapes (the seeded variety).

Supplies:

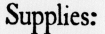

Plastic Cable Ties x 12, medium-sized

Long Paper Clips x 2

Rubber Bands x 3

Plastic Spoon or Spork

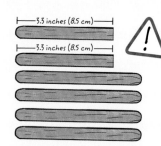

— 3.3 inches (8.5 cm) —

— 3.3 inches (8.5 cm) —

Six craft sticks make up the frame. Cut two lengths of 3.3 inches (8.5 cm) with heavy scissors.

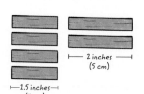

— 2 inches (5 cm) —

— 1.5 inches (4 cm) —

Six craft stick sections make the two crosspieces. Cut four lengths of 1.5 inches (4 cm) and two lengths of 2 inches (5 cm).

Tools:

Duct Tape

Scissors

Craft Knife

Wood Glue

0.6 inch (1.5 cm) 0.6 inch (1.5 cm)

You will need the body of a ballpoint pen. Cut off two lengths, each 0.6 inch (1.5 cm) long.

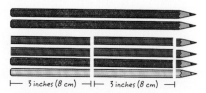

— 3 inches (8 cm) — — 3 inches (8 cm) —

You will need six pencils. Two are full-length. Cut the tips off the other four, and cut down to 3 inches (8 cm).

Instructions
STAGE 1

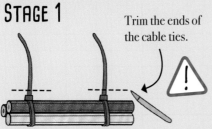

Trim the ends of the cable ties.

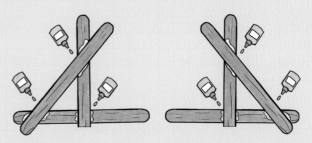

1 The front and back of the base are bundles of three pencil sections. Hold them together with cable ties pulled tight.

2 The sides are made as mirror images of each other. For each side, glue together two uncut craft sticks to one 3.3-inch (8.5-cm) section.

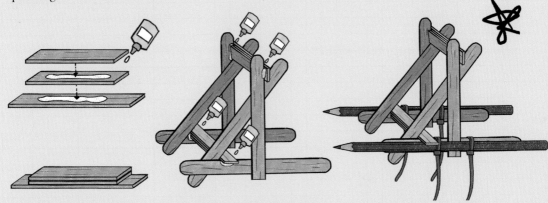

3 For each crosspiece, glue two short pieces together. Glue the new piece centrally to a longer piece. Allow the glue to dry.

4 Glue the frame sides together as shown. Remember they are mirror images of each other. Again, allow the glue to dry thoroughly before the next step.

5 Fix one of the pencils to the outside of the frame with cable ties. Repeat on the other side, making sure the pencils are lined up.

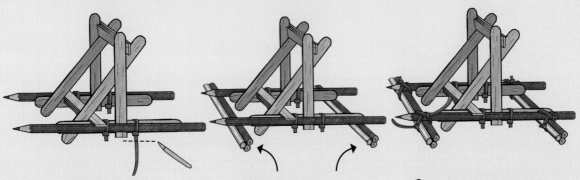

6 Trim the cable tie ends.

7 Position the two end pieces as shown.

8 Attach the end pieces with cable ties pulled tight.

STAGE 2

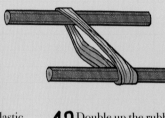

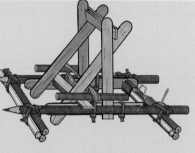

9 To make the trigger, shape one paper clip as shown, as you thread it through the short ballpoint pen sections.

10 Secure these sections in place with duct tape.

11 Fold out and shape a paper clip to make the hook that connects to the trigger.

STAGE 3

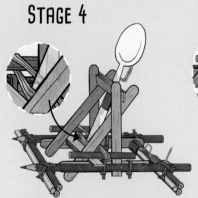

12 Cut the handle of the plastic spoon, so the bowl extends past the catapult frame when flat. Tape the hook to the spoon.

13 Double up the rubber bands and loop them around the two remaining 3-inch (8-cm) pencil stubs.

14 Thread them into place in the frame as shown. This is a little tricky so take care and keep trying!

STAGE 4

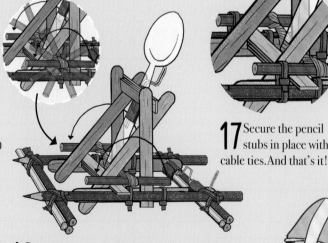

15 Fit the end of the spoon into the rubber bands.

17 Secure the pencil stubs in place with cable ties. And that's it!

16 Tighten up the rubber bands by slightly turning the pencil stubs. If the rubber bands are already tight, a half-turn will do the job!

STAGE 5

Ready! Aim! Launch!

Pull the trigger down to release the catapult.

18 Pull the spoon down and engage the trigger hook. Place a grape in the spoon and you're ready to attack!

Early Catapults

Large catapults dominated warfare and helped ancient empires expand. The spring mechanism enabled the machines to pick off enemy troops from a distance, pinning them to the ground with long, heavy bolts or arrows. The balls they fired could fell ranks of soldiers at a range of 1,300 feet (400 m).

BALLISTA

Looking like a giant fixed crossbow, the ballista had two firing arms drawn back by a rope to release its weapons. For this mini-version, blunt the end of your projectile with an eraser before pinging it across the room.

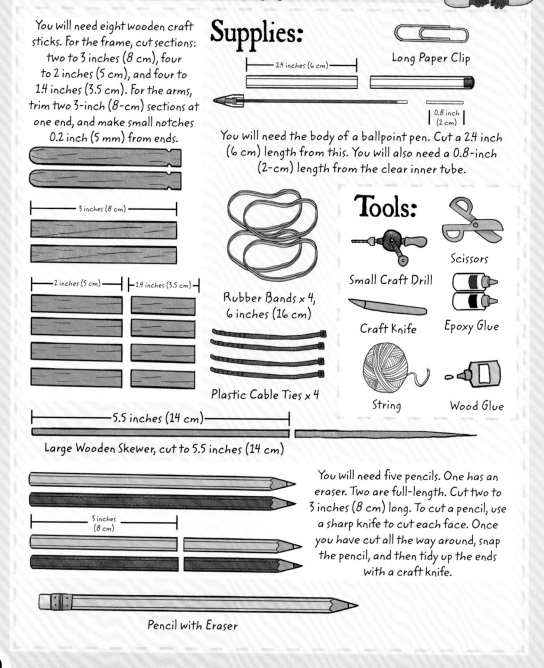

You will need eight wooden craft sticks. For the frame, cut sections: two to 3 inches (8 cm), four to 2 inches (5 cm), and four to 1.4 inches (3.5 cm). For the arms, trim two 3-inch (8-cm) sections at one end, and make small notches 0.2 inch (5 mm) from ends.

3 inches (8 cm)

2 inches (5 cm)   1.4 inches (3.5 cm)

Supplies:

2.4 inches (6 cm)

Long Paper Clip

0.8 inch (2 cm)

You will need the body of a ballpoint pen. Cut a 2.4 inch (6 cm) length from this. You will also need a 0.8-inch (2-cm) length from the clear inner tube.

Rubber Bands x 4, 6 inches (16 cm)

Plastic Cable Ties x 4

Tools:

Small Craft Drill

Scissors

Craft Knife

Epoxy Glue

String

Wood Glue

5.5 inches (14 cm)

Large Wooden Skewer, cut to 5.5 inches (14 cm)

3 inches (8 cm)

You will need five pencils. One has an eraser. Two are full-length. Cut two to 3 inches (8 cm) long. To cut a pencil, use a sharp knife to cut each face. Once you have cut all the way around, snap the pencil, and then tidy up the ends with a craft knife.

Pencil with Eraser

Instructions

Stage 1

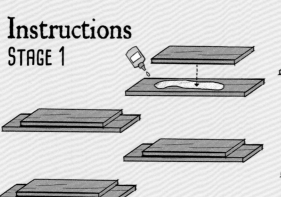

1 Make the four uprights by gluing a 1.4-inch (3.5-cm) piece of craft stick centrally to a 2-inch (5-cm) piece, using wood glue. Allow the glue to dry.

2 Place a 3-inch (8-cm) section centrally on the shorter upright and glue in place. Allow to dry and repeat on the other side.

Stage 2

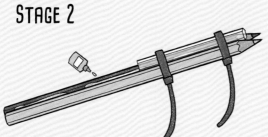

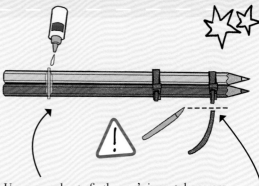

3 Glue together two full-length pencils with wood glue. Line up the pen's outer tube with the pencil points, then tie the bundle together tightly with two cable ties.

4 Use epoxy glue to fix the pen's inner tube across the two pencils on the opposite side from the pen's outer tube, roughly 1.2 inches (3 cm) from the ends. Trim the cable ties.

Stage 3

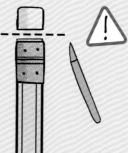

5 To make the bolt, cut off the eraser as close to the pencil as possible.

6 Drill a small hole in the eraser with the craft drill. Fit it to the end of the cut section of the skewer. Glue in place with epoxy glue.

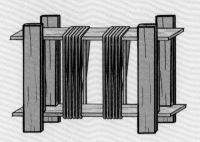

7 Wrap two pairs of rubber bands three times each around the frame, positioning them as shown.

8 Fit the notched arms into the rubber bands, adding a twist as shown. Make sure that the arms twang up against the frame when you release them.

9 Fit the pencil and pen tube bundle into the bottom of the frame with the pen's outer tube on top.

10 Fasten it in place with two cable ties crossed over (shown here from underneath). Trim the ends.

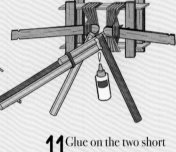

11 Glue on the two short pencil pieces using epoxy glue. This makes the ballista's legs.

12 To string up the ballista, cut a length of string slightly longer than the width of the ballista arms. Tie it on at one notch.

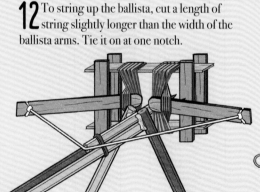

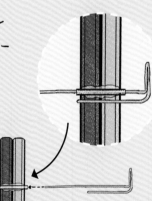

13 Fit the string around the pen tube and tie it on at the other notch. The string must remain under tension.

14 To make the trigger, unfold a large paper clip and form it into the shape shown.

15 Thread it into the pen's inner tube on the underside of the pencils.

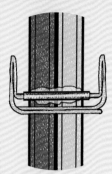

16 Fold the wire around from the other side to make the shape in the next step.

17 The trigger should lift up like this.

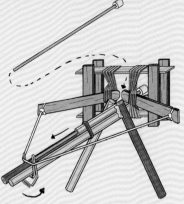

18 Lift and hold the trigger, pull back the string, and hook it over the trigger. Thread the bolt into the tube and engage it with the string.

Launch!

MEDIEVAL BALLISTA

In early warfare, both attackers and defenders used ballistas. They had a great firing range from castle ramparts, and were mounted on swiveling platforms for shooting accuracy. An attacking army might mount smaller ballistas on carts for mobile weapons on the battlefield.

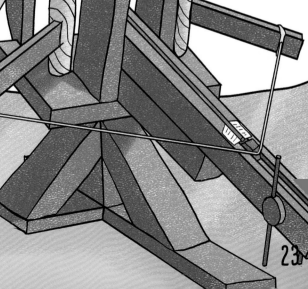

Air Musket

Some historic weapons used air, not fire, power to shoot a projectile. The eighteenth-century air rifle was relatively quiet and caused no smoke screen. Yours won't have a smoking barrel either—just a puff of sugar from marshmallow projectiles.

Supplies:

Cardboard Tube from Aluminum Foil Box, 11.5 inches (30 cm)

Mini Marshmallows

Wooden Spoon Handle or Dowel, 13 inches (33 cm) long

Washcloth

Netting from a Fruit Bag

Mesh Bath Sponge

Plastic Bag

Tools:

Duct Tape

Craft Knife

Instructions
STAGE 1

1 Pull a piece of netting over the end of the tube that will form the barrel. Tape the netting to the tube. This will stop the marshmallows from falling into the air bag.

2 Cut off the string of the mesh bath sponge. Unravel it.

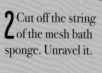

3 Wrap a piece of the plastic bag around the mesh bath sponge so it fits loosely inside.

STAGE 2

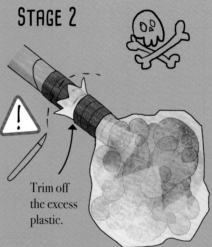

Trim off the excess plastic.

4 Push the netted end of the barrel into the plastic bag and tape around it. This makes a sealed bag which blows air through the barrel when it is squeezed.

5 To make the ramrod, cut the handle from a wooden spoon or use a dowel. Scrunch up a piece of a washcloth into a ball so it fits inside the barrel's open end.

6 Wrap another piece of washcloth around the ball and place over the end of the spoon handle or dowel.

STAGE 3

7 Fit the ramrod inside and tape the washcloth firmly around the ramrod. Trim off the excess washcloth.

8 Load the barrel with tasty mini marshmallows and gently push them into place with the ramrod.

9 Aim the barrel, then push down on the bag. The springiness of the bath sponge will reinflate the bag afterwards.

AIR POWER

The most famous air rifle was the Girandoni model adopted by the Austrian Army from 1780 to 1815. It arrived in the United States in 1803, and one was carried by Meriwether Lewis and William Clark on their expedition to map the western states.

Simple Catapult

The Romans found the basic catapult design so effective that their engineers just kept making and improving it. This catapult is made from mint boxes and is perfect for launching mini marshmallows.

Supplies:

Duct Tape

Mini Marshmallows

Plastic Mint Boxes x 4

Rubber Bands x 2

Plastic Spoon or Spork

Instructions
Stage 1

1 Tape together three of the boxes (as shown).

2 Lay them flat and tape the fourth box across the top.

3 Wrap two rubber bands around the two boxes that stick out (as shown).

STAGE 2

4 Thread in the spoon or spork, with the concave side facing away from you. Twist the rubber bands around the handle as you insert it.

Completed Catapult

Aim... Launch!

5 Pull down the spoon, load up and . . .

ROMAN CATAPULT

When the Romans first invaded Britain in 43 CE, the standard bolt-shooting catapult was the Scorpio, operated by individual soldiers. Its force was provided by a winch or pole tightly wound with rope made of animal sinew (tissue). This created the spring effect. It was praised by Julius Caesar for its accuracy.

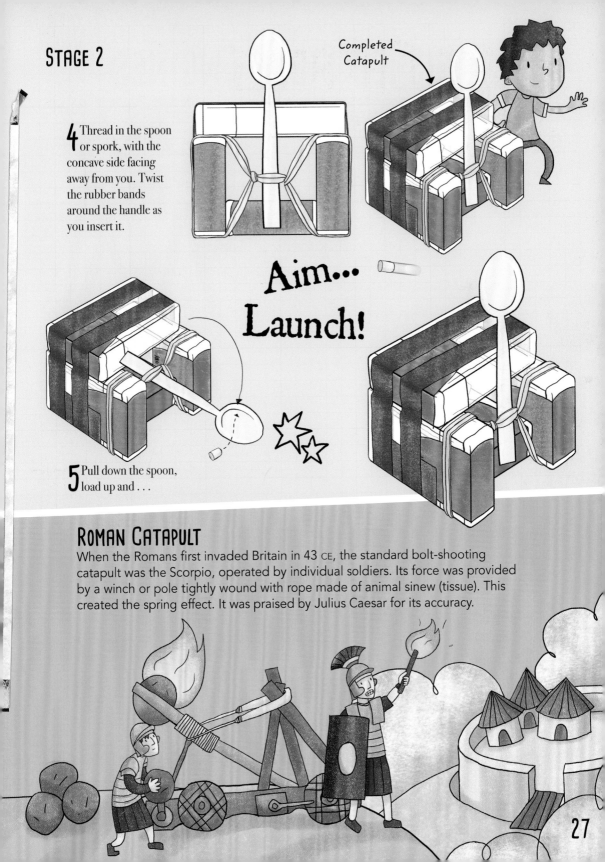

THE FINISHED SIEGE ENGINES

These amazing models show just how impressive these weapons were in ancient and medieval times. They were used to weaken the enemy or bring down walls.

Trebuchet

Based On: Medieval trebuchet

First Invented In: China

Range: 100–200 feet (30–61 m)

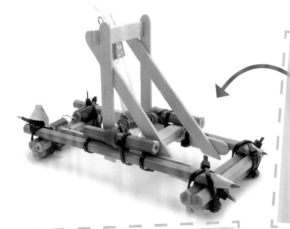

Catapult

Based On: Torsion catapult

Invented By: Ancient Greeks or Romans

Powered By: Coiled rope spring mechanism

Air Musket

Based On: Girandoni air rifle

Invented By: Bartholomaus Girandoni, around 1778

Original Size: 4 feet (1.2 m)

Onager

Based On: Onager of around 250 BCE

Invented By: Ancient Romans

Missiles: Rocks up to 150 pounds (70 kg)

Simple Catapult

Based On: Scorpio catapult

Invented By: Ancient Greeks

Payload: Bolts

Ballista

Based On: Ballista of around 400 BCE

Invented By: Ancient Greeks

Missiles: Stones and flaming bolts

SIEGE ENGINES IN HISTORY

These thundering weapons were used in warfare for centuries.
Travel back in time and discover them in action . . .

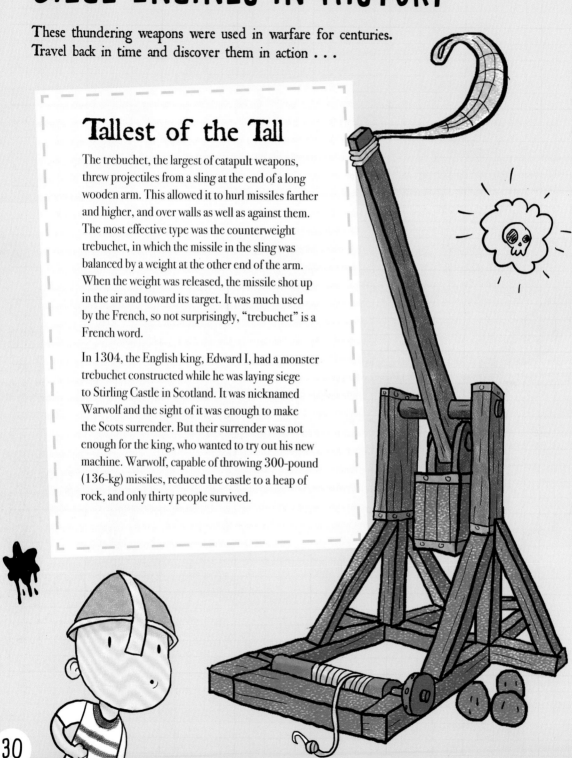

Tallest of the Tall

The trebuchet, the largest of catapult weapons, threw projectiles from a sling at the end of a long wooden arm. This allowed it to hurl missiles farther and higher, and over walls as well as against them. The most effective type was the counterweight trebuchet, in which the missile in the sling was balanced by a weight at the other end of the arm. When the weight was released, the missile shot up in the air and toward its target. It was much used by the French, so not surprisingly, "trebuchet" is a French word.

In 1304, the English king, Edward I, had a monster trebuchet constructed while he was laying siege to Stirling Castle in Scotland. It was nicknamed Warwolf and the sight of it was enough to make the Scots surrender. But their surrender was not enough for the king, who wanted to try out his new machine. Warwolf, capable of throwing 300-pound (136-kg) missiles, reduced the castle to a heap of rock, and only thirty people survived.

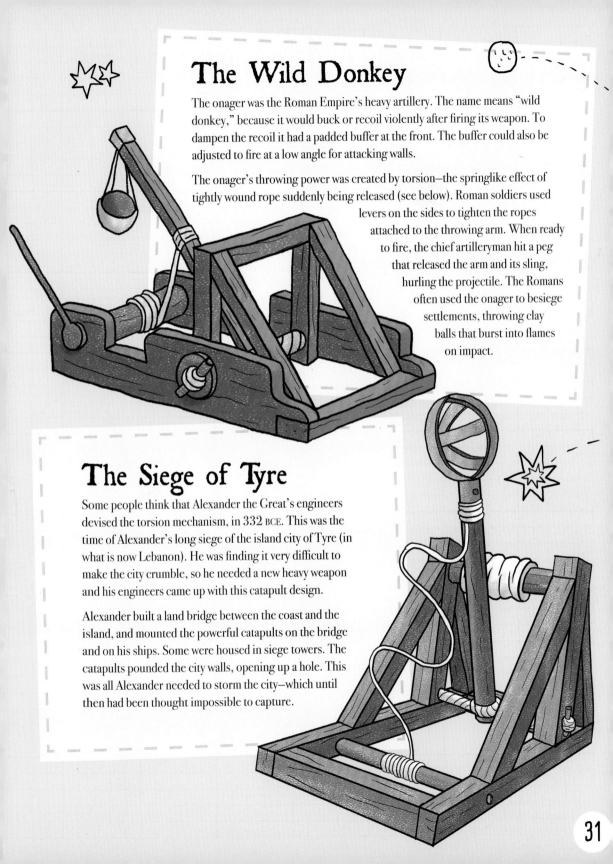

The Wild Donkey

The onager was the Roman Empire's heavy artillery. The name means "wild donkey," because it would buck or recoil violently after firing its weapon. To dampen the recoil it had a padded buffer at the front. The buffer could also be adjusted to fire at a low angle for attacking walls.

The onager's throwing power was created by torsion—the springlike effect of tightly wound rope suddenly being released (see below). Roman soldiers used levers on the sides to tighten the ropes attached to the throwing arm. When ready to fire, the chief artilleryman hit a peg that released the arm and its sling, hurling the projectile. The Romans often used the onager to besiege settlements, throwing clay balls that burst into flames on impact.

The Siege of Tyre

Some people think that Alexander the Great's engineers devised the torsion mechanism, in 332 BCE. This was the time of Alexander's long siege of the island city of Tyre (in what is now Lebanon). He was finding it very difficult to make the city crumble, so he needed a new heavy weapon and his engineers came up with this catapult design.

Alexander built a land bridge between the coast and the island, and mounted the powerful catapults on the bridge and on his ships. Some were housed in siege towers. The catapults pounded the city walls, opening up a hole. This was all Alexander needed to storm the city—which until then had been thought impossible to capture.

INDEX

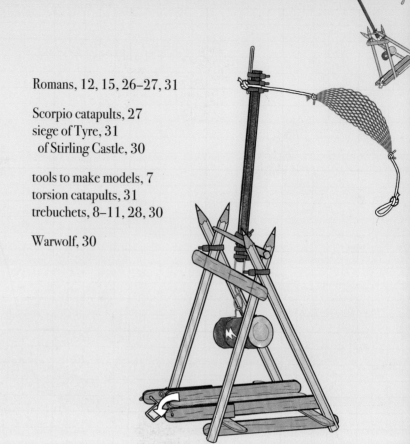

THE AUTHOR

Rob Ives is a United Kingdom-based designer and paper engineer.
He began making cardboard models as a math and science teacher,
and then was asked to create two books of models. His published
titles include *Paper Models that Rock!* and *Paper Automata*. He
specializes in paper animations and projects, and often visits schools
to talk about design technology and demonstrate his models.

THE ARTIST

John Paul de Quay is an illustrator with a BSc in Biology from
the University of Sussex, United Kingdom, and a postgraduate
certificate in animation from the University of the West of England.
He devotes his spare time to growing chili peppers, perfecting his
plan for a sustainable future, and caring for a small plastic dinosaur.
He has three pet squid that live in the bath, which makes drawing in
ink quite economical . . .

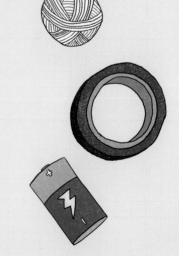